INTO THE LIGHT
- A Collection of Poems & Quotes

Tiyiselani Tlhavani

Publisher: www.sakurabookpublishing.com
alta@sakurabookpublishing.com
Cover design, Editing and Interior design: Alta H Haffner

ISBN: 978-1-0370-8945-9(print)

   978-1-0370-8946-6(e-book)

POETRY AND QUOTES

Title: INTO THE LIGHT-
Anthology of Poems & Quotes
Genre: Consciousness By
Tiyiselani Tlhavani

Thank you

It's gratitude I feel, towards this very life! The lessons you taught me, I see that life comes in packages, not individualism. So I learn to share, kindly wholeheartedly.

"I'm not of the hate nation,
Just set my spirit on fire
And see me rise and rise"
~ Tiyiselani Tlhavani

About the Author

Tiyiselani Tlhavani

Tiyiselane Tlhavani is a poet who weaves words to evoke awareness through the gentle whispers of intuition.

Born in Giyani, Limpopo. South Africa. He attended school at Giyani High, then later completed a Bcom in Tourism Management at the university of Venda.

Tiyiselane is a full-time hairdresser and a part-time administration clerk at a local school.

" Into the Light " is his debut book, a poetry anthology that invites listeners to the subtle language of intuition, guiding readers toward greater self-awareness and inner wisdom.

Into the Light

From darkness we came
We travelled thousands of miles
Over 9 months
And Into the light were born
And life were crowned
To witness this glorious light
That satisfied our eyes to see
And our hearts to feel.

Music

True music
to be sang
played
and listened to

Is the music
that touch
heal
nurture well-being

music
that forgives
and forget
pain and suffering
of hate that divide
our heart apart.

True music
Is the rhythm
of heart
A soul that flows
A mind that finds.
Harmony within
and spread to the terrified world.

Black skin

Not a colour but melanin
Of royalty
Anointed by almighty light
The sun's lover
Kisses all day long.

Fully packed with DNA
Information that began
And keeps the world evolve

You astrologist, chemist, mathematician,
and farmers.
Founding the universe.

You're the dark night
That celebrate the stars
A secret where all source
Surfing for Life.
Myelinated Forever And ever Amen Ra
Dark I AM
Light I live

Listen Intuition

Everything that you hear
That does not spring from your soul,
Are gossips that wants to distract you from the Way
And all will lead to your lowest, through limits,
Boundaries and gravity that denies you evolution (Realization)
Serving you believes than knowing
and fear been your burden till death.

But listening from the soul
Enhances one into LOVE,
Serving knowledge and silencing fear into emptiness
Aligning you to equality with the universe.

This is your original position within the system,
You're a star that shines at night
and a flower that blooms in spring.
Realize this! that you're the missing piece
To make up HEAVEN

Soul Purpose

It is the heart that feels,
Through intuition calmly
Purporting harmony and knowledge
To make the world a better stay.

The heart is conscious
and willing on high purpose.
As it seeks to install order
To the terrified world
Filled with tribulations

But to a mind that is believing
while doubting,
it does not care about the heart that feels.
The egoistic mind selfishly
wants to control the world
Disregarding unity that the heart feels
and alignment of human chakras.

As the mind continues to plunge
the world into chaos
Through dangerous discoveries
And democracy that is filled
with immoral choices.

A soul that flows these magnitudes,
Like a stardust sparking life into this universe.
Soul wants to break free
from the believe system(World)
That is powered by the mind.

Like a meditating monk
harnessing silence in the mountains of Tibet.
The soul appeals to the mind
and the heart to get along,
So to ascend humanity to the divine purpose.

The day I was born

From these light rays we descended
And below we took cover!
Broke my eyes open,
That's my mind being sold to the world.
There's no time for thyself now,
Get busy as a bee.

Interacting, transacting with machines,
That credit profit & debit love!
My heart so hollow now,
This greed as dug out this precious feeling.

So I'm named, attached with a code!
It has nothing to do with me,
But only just a reference
That I'm a property of the Beast
That ran us on believes,
Making us candidate of hell.

But the all-seeing eye,
See-through love.
As I met with divine spirit,
That fed into my nostrils,

As I catch life & along with divine interaction,
I see, I feel, hear, smell and then touch!
I'm for a deeper exploration,
Than this shallow minded programming

Against self

The bullets are raining down
And it looks not safe.
People keep closing their eyes for mercy
But it all ended six feet under.
For these lands there's an enemy
That keeps on charging.

Bodies are laying low.
No imagination to spark them.
For fear has lamented in each one of us.
And the rise of the sun?
Still brought no smile.

We are choked to believe!
Away from Feeling that knowing.
Calling us born again.
Mocking the womb that shaped the earth.

We do have power to finish,
Put all sadness away
But we have forgotten,
The time Ubuntu was caring,
When the stars help us to realize
and the moon revived our souls.

Our hearts are too broken,
Into pieces, beyond repair!
by mind that feeding pain & fear.
And now, our eyes are becoming!
Like those of an widow.
It's war against self.

→>>>>>> <<<<<<-

Finding you.

Standing on the cross roads,
I'm crossed, moaning!
Life's faded meaning.
Nor purpose I lead.

So what's up for grabs?
In tapping into my flows?
The gifts I preserve?

There's a moment of silence,
And thunder! to strike the skies.
I'm attentive to receive!

Be generous about being yourself in this life,
So that in return?
The universe would give you undivided attention, We call Love.
The universe is an exploring expressing body of souls,
For those bodies that can openly confess their WITHIN.

Because WITHOUT is a distraction.
Pretending to be self.
Serving deception.
As you simply hide,
From the universe that wants to reveal/pour you goodness.

FEAR! Is another raging war!
That is denying you abundance from this caring universe,
Because fear is an intimidation of your becoming.

See also life in this universe is an opportunity to learn,
discover and embrace love that invited you here.
See you don't stand here alone.
There are thousands behind, Encouraging!
As you move towards self-discovery.

See you do not owe, no one, Nothing!
Your everything.
Genesis and into the end.
Partake in gratitude.
You're guided.
So keep calm.

~Do not fear to mirror yourself out of that mind,
Because the heart is always ready to
blossom you out of that limitation~

Believe & Knowledge

Began to see the true nature of these lies,
called believes.
Believes are sickness, ignorance that
denies us realization.
Leaving many in disappointment.
Waiting for no arrival
Knocking for no opening.

It's a slaves mentality, brought by the masters,
To keep slaves off- balance..
Its fear mongering, mind prison cell,
condemning expression of a mind.

You're the saviour of yourself from this force that
consumes you.
Making you to see, feel, hear which is not,
So to formally introduce you into this great lie
that moves around contaminating your chakras.
Hindering you to receive/ connect from harmony.

Acknowledge that knowledge is the light that let you through
many closed gates,
to see beyond believes, answers that frees us home,
light we belong.

Knowledge is a beauty,
A crown of a king,
Ruling & understanding the true divine nature of things.

So fight! Steadily, grounding yourself in this nature,
Your invisible on this weapon that defeat fear of death,
Crowning you immunity.
This battle only begins from within because this without
attacks this within.

You are the victim then, defend "cover your heart from scavengers
that seeks your wealth",
Standing by within, Listening to that small
voice, that seek to share some light in your path.
You are a gift to this beautiful healing mother-earth.

Understand also, that love is fair, balance,
A perfection for you to become God,
Is appreciating & freely distributed to every
being, particle that makes up the earth.

We live in the land ruled by many lights,
Sun, moon, stars to make sure that beauty
shines out from deep places unknown by the
mind, to attract/ invite many rainbows of butterflies..
Mmmhhhh!!! its goodness, jubilation
Fight!, revolt this shouting noises on your ears,
that denies you hearing from your beloved ones.

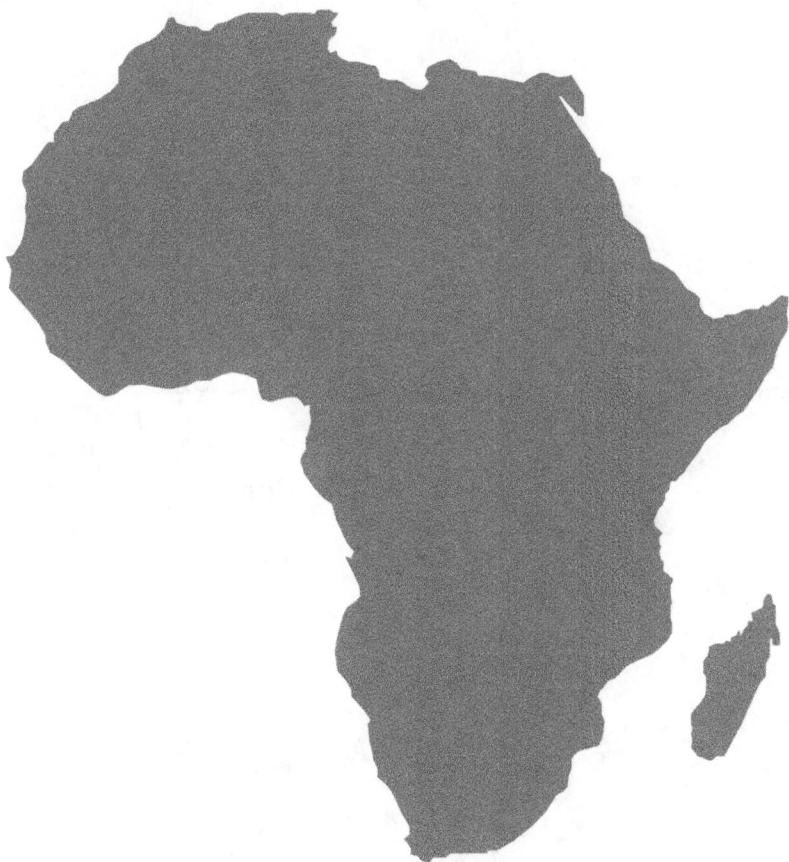

In our heart we knew
But in our mind we doubted
And in our eyes we wept!
~ Tiyiselani Tlhavani

Heart

Still standing right here,
at your door to paradise.
Knock, knock! knock!
Been knocking here since like its forever!
Still no answer to open, to free you through to the
other side of your dreams.
My rhythm don't change
I keep playing, drumming the very same beat
that your life gratitude to.
Shaking you up, revving you warm to embrace
these dimensions.

I'm So feeling, feeling infused with knowledge, knowing
calm from your deepest sense that calls you home.
Calling you to feel
Those gifts that are up for grabs,
For you to smile out that happiness,
To explore you out from this moaning, confusing places
that keep on stealing,
Promising you what they are not.

Listen, feel that I'm the way, portal to your deepest self.
To purpose you to find that hidden treasure in silence,
Unimagined places by the mind that keeps on changing.
How in the universe can you find/know me through
your untrusted friend(mind)
That always land you in trouble after trouble,
A friend that keeps on talking, capturing you with beliefs
that are strange to you.

Still knocking right here at your door to paradise.
Witness me innocent in the eyes of a child, that glows
out heaven,
To invite you to join many ascending angels of skies
working-out these stars,
that are celebrated by the night.
I'm just like a child that approaches life gentler
but quicker
to fulfil its curiosity.
This feeling on silence is calm, behold all heritage of
your being is
served at your attentiveness.
Let me be free to saviour this body from
these en-slavers
that keep on repeating mistakes,
Cries and pains that distance you out of divinity.

~'Shouting out The Heart, Possessing Love'~

My condolences

My dear self
Africa who use to roar
Drumming celebrations
Kudu horn we United

She's flowing waters
Rivers of quench
Forests of immune
Harvest of health
Earth the mother
Life she crown

Tell me about
UBUNTU
That single word
Describe a kingdom
From busy bees
She built pyramids
That drips wisdom
We sweetened

My condolences to her Today
She lost her heart
Connection to self
She got no health to consume
Only sickness to maintain

She forgotten life
And forgave death
And now her womb
Drop a tomb

illusion

Welcome to illusion
Its magic
Its slaves the mind, and troubles the body.
We are here, we are played by these great manipulators,
Mind grabbers that steals us from freedom to captivity.

Captivity of vulnerability from these priests that keep on
terrifying our souls with fires of hell,
Politicians that keep on
capturing us with lies of no breakthrough
And businessman's that keep on selling us,
us the heritage of mother earth.
They are worms in our minds that eat the conscious in us,
love in us.
That make us to see through the veil of lies.
knowing hate, pain through their voice,
making us to forget many of our beloved ones
While they keep on pulling many of ourselves.
You see these machines, this technology
and the music you hear,
It's a magnet, a curse that thieves us from
our mothers arms.
Stationing us watching time passing around &around,
Dazing us to a deep sleep of endless nightmares.

Once upon a time, in this Jewish man's circus.
There was a great deception,
that caught everybody not blinking but believing,
Consuming and praising the shadows of the dark.
A show that shrink morals and steal more to the heart.
A show that get people to forget their past while
killing their presence and selling them the future!

See my people walking, mindless
zombies obeying mirrors,
Always driving on a right hand lane either left
lead to no destination.
Yes, Seeing is Believing but understand that
Feeling is Knowing.
You see these manipulators that separate
the mind from the heart,
Setting the mind in strange places
where it cannot remember who it was
"knowledge of self", Leaving the heart in lone,
longing for it loved one.

See mind remains as the only part most abused,
Destroyed by this entertainment of immorality,
That set many bodies in depression.
Living in the matrix that shows no love
but profit, survival.
Matrix has no feelings, emotions,
It's a heartless wolf that tears us down.
Judging, Prosecuting love & finally rising the beast,
That would scatter many souls astray.

Tree

When they came,
They found us already in love,
Bonded so thick to our beloved earth.
How our roots so deep,
We knitted this earth below.
Stronger to hold life still!
Above these grounds.

We are here!
Rocking and rolling,
Seasons changing faces,
To embrace us with moments
Of blooming gratitude.
Where birds and butterflies propelled gloriously
And landed with thanks.

As they tread upon!
They printed shame,
Shepherds of death
That demotivated our history with the ancients.
Jealousy is their lifeline.
Exploring our downfall.

Even though they saw how desperate life means to us,
They continued to suck our life from our beloved.
No matter how hard we tried to hold on!
They would send us bulldozers
To kill us without taking our last feel,
Of this blowing wind.

The ticket

I'm riding on a bus.
And I'm full of suspicion.
These men have no trust.
It's sort of sad,
like I booked myself a ticket of no return.

Their eyes are cursing!
Calling an end to every beginning.
My mind grief perforated.
By this secret game in shadows,
Where men in long hooded robes,

Hold a circle of tribulations,
Involving children to evolve themselves.

By the window I peer,
It's a dream out there!
Touch of sun rays,
Stars creative art on this dark nights,
Drew a line that compliments Life.

I'm in the lost world.
No one comes alive.
Infiltrated by very same old criminal.
As the great heist progresses,
Disarming the heartbeat,
As oxygen revolves dust!

I did tried to close eyes for escape,
But this unapologetic hand of enemy,
Keep stretching judgement.
It's a ticket of no return.

Silence is the frequency of knowledge,
That meditators seek to listen.
So they are let to know the message
from the divine. ~ Tiyiselani Nhavani

In This World

In this world of light pushed by the dark.
In skies of sun and moon battling to be the
superstar of the age.
In a platform where technology battles to be nature and
opinion seeking to be fact.

In this world of ceaseless and endless struggle.
Where the mind wants to govern the body
through believe of an eye,
than a heart that seeks to rule through
a feel of knowledge.
Where also Love is not discovered through
a feel of heart
but through a see of an eye.

In a time, where the mind is applauded for
its dangerous discovery,
A world where people close their eyes when
seeking life and mercy,
Then opening to these beautiful forests
filled with miracles.

In a world where bodies are falling and too many
machines are rising!
In a space where humans are consulting robots.

In a world of too much-waked eyes but shut souls,
Where false faces are smiled at, while pure
faces are frowned at.
Where love is stabbed by an arrow while
hate is cuddled for the next war.
Where greed is invested in the community
by the businessman.

In this world where light finds and darkness hides.
In a world where heads and tails are from the same coin.
Left and right hand are from the same body,
And Good and then Evil are from the same man.

In this world where darkness also loved to be Light.
Where pain defines the next smile,
Where demons in veils are praised for their magic.

In this world where many sold their kindness for money
and Zombies they became as they continue
to seek the blood of the innocents.
In a world where people show emotions and
sympathize with a TV program.

In a world where street light describes safety
while broken one fears it away.
In a world where hands work together for
profit than joining for unity.

In a world where the mirror defines the self.

A world where many are guarded by fear rather than
guided by love.
In a world filled with many lights but that
do not lead to any discovery.

In a world where dreams are sold over the counter!
And pain & suffering are advertised for their next profit.

In a world where Love is choking! while hate is breeding!
A world said that one man felt unbearable pain just
to save our lives,
While also indeed is the mother for 9 months who bled this
unbearable to give us Life.

In this world of many thoughts & sights,
Where life dances to the rhythm of the heartbeat.
In a society that advances in reverse psychology.
Where poisonous foods are termed Junk food.
In a world where people come in unity to celebrate a disease.

In this World! where I will die and Resurrect in my dreams.

Into the dark

Dark in here, cold.
Wolves revving! owls watching.
Fear is the veil
and Everything looks consuming.

Sshhhhhh!!
This silence is a snare,
Trapping my soul to the deep.
tap tap tap!
Footsteps surrounding,
Crawling sounds of no rhythm.
Everything is disheartening

Night falling!
So pitch that no eye can see
So blind that no light can be saved.
Body shrinking heat.
Cold eating to the bone.

I'm so disabled now.
Only heart beating attentively.
In this worse situation,
That is so sad to imagine.

Something crawling there,
With a sound that blanked my mind.
How horrible is this!
Being trapped in pain that cannot be wept.

In this deep darkness of fear,
My mind came so defeated.
But only my soul stayed still,
Calming this suspense.

There's two ways

There are two ways only.
To travel our life path.
To reach us to our purpose or chaos.
But I consider a little that there's only one way.
To travel your life path.
But since you're a citizen of choice.
Let's say there are two ways.
So you can have a choice to make.

There's a way of a HEART
And a way of MIND.
This was supposed to be a major subject
To be taught,
But only if we ever had schools,
But since we have concentration camps,
We never knew it!

So let me be of an honour
As I write, to kindly advice you
On either side of your choice.
So you cannot be surprised
On what to be discussed
On your meeting!

I indulge
Follow me on the MIND path!
To the chaos that was once quoted as hell!
You are judgemental, doubtful
That's hateful!
So you're a sick somebody now.
Cheating on thyself.

Your very decision is executed by the mind,
That's a traveling speed, it does not belong.
So you became a believer! That I'm aware!

That's why you have no knowledge
Because you go to the world
Following the command of a man,
Underestimating your willpower!
So you bow to the enemy.
Where fear is hosting.
So there's a fight within.

You worried I know
Just have that forgiveness
You healing!
As I write you to a path of a HEART
You're a flow of abundance
Even though lonely sometimes.
Rest assured.
Smile is cheap
You feel knowledge
Beautifully
Embracing your dreams.
Love is energy
You connect light
Shine brighter!
That's the purpose
Your destiny.

In mind we are different
In heart we are same,
The mind can judge
but heart cannot.
~ Tiyiselani Tlhavani

Not enough

Why say you're enough!
While you haven't reflected yourself unto the stars!
That wonders on the path of your only purpose.
Why say you're at peace while you haven't gaze
upon rising & falling sun for harmony.
Why say you are safe, while in the world of tribulations,
Where fear comes alive to haunt all the good times,
Where all your gifts and talents are undermined by careers.

Why say you're enough when you can't let your
heart roam it's desires and the mind to reach
your destiny.
Why say you're at unity, while you can't barely
foot mother earth connection.
Why say you're fulfilled, when you can't let the
rainbow fills the spectrum of your life.

Why your supposed friends are your enemies?
Why hate is your loved one?
Why do dreams lurk nightmares?
Why look outside for answers, satisfaction to a
the time that is passing,
Expiring and leaving you worn out?

Why don't you say:
You have had enough of foreign identities
that do not define.

Why don't you take time?
A moment in silence.
To find art in your darkness.
To be the artist of your Light.
You're enough.

In the Name

When they came from our shores,
They were like ants lined in dedication
And in commitment to their project of harvest.
So as far as we looked, we never minded the minors,
but as closer they got then we realized that we
got the major ones.

They were rising in giant,
with a written name on their foreheads
And a tongue that seems to shoot us at heart.
We tried to raise our shields but we're heartbroken,
We're not going to be still anymore.

We begin to fall on our heads
While some broke into their knees,
As they join the name to continue killing one of their own.

We felt great shame brought by this exodus,
Being taken out of our hearts and to a name that is
always judging, and prosecuting.

We did stand this trial.
Rising accused of being in possession of demons,
And the name became Revving!!
Fiery in the eyes, just like fires of hell that
began to haunt our spirits
And sorrow we bore and in-depth with the earth.

Sleeping

I'm swinging slowly.
A Lullaby into my deep,
place of boundless free will.
Regrets unforeseen here.
Everything is taking place quietly,
Nothing will ever hurt you.

You were the separation all along,
And now you came uniting dimensions into one
Love, one authority
One rhythm.
That let you dance to eternity.

Your Pure, unique and untouchable formation.
Like a star that shines from million miles away,
Carrying attentions of many ancient souls.

You have forgotten all pain,
Worries brought by the day.
You're the real incarnate now
Manifest that perfection.
Turn this world upright
Let it align with harmony
You came across the thick line
That bolds the MILKYWAY,
It's the right direction.
Shooting straight home,
Taurus, Leo, Aries, cancer etc
All we descended.

Who we used to be.

You see us now,
we are not ourselves
We are their choice,
We are products,
we are sold, traded.
Our divine mind is stolen & kept by the evil master.
For our mind was courage that set us as kings & queens.

They found us gathered around fires, sharing
tales in the night of moon & stars.
We never feared but we always strive and celebrated life.
These stars and moon acknowledge,
Who we are!
Our days were brightly shone by this African sun,
that seems to love, kiss this African skin.

We raced and battled on who would count all these stars.
We raced on who would wake first to feel the
rays of this morning star.
We were courageous.
Were curious to know.
We walked this earth barefooted.
Thorns never bothered us, for they knew were
together in DNA with the earth.

The moon & stars spectated us,
As we dance to this rhythm of the African
cowhide drum, that scattered spirits all over
the forests and skies.
For this cowhide drum, animals & birds in the
field felt touched, and harmonized as they sang
joyously the next morning.
Animals giving birth, rivers flowed and we harvested
as the rain came.

Washing always worries of yesterday.
Quenching us with new knowledge.
Sun shining us with hope,
Strengthening us in this new beginning.

For this cowhide drum was the gospel of our souls.
Play that cowhide drum & you will realize.
Play it once and you will find your missing self,
Beat that drum once & again and Africa
will unite in harmony.
For it is the rhythm of our souls.
For the sun sparks our souls
And the earth hold our bodies together!
Let us once n again ride this universe.

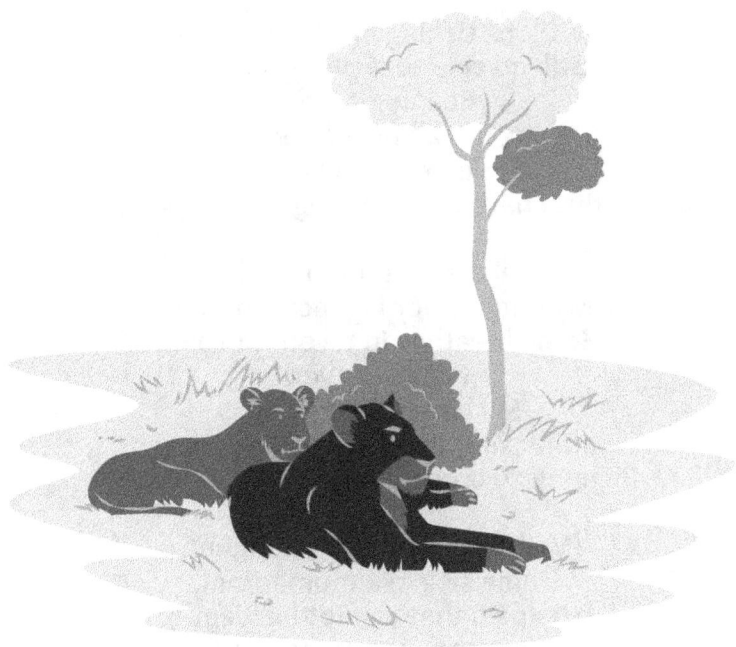

Can't sleep

Night had fall.
Body retire!
Eyes are begotten Chinese.
But shy to say goodnight.
So I'm vigilant.
For what? I do not know.
So I'm tossing & turning.

Clock ticking is teasing me.
Still no side to view my dreams.
Bed don't hurt.
It's a queens bed.
For baby sleep i guess.
But i have been tossing & turning.

Still can't figure out why,
My mind is not in place with me.
Some breathes in favour of calm.
Not there yet!
My head still crazing..
Knocking the deaf man's door.
Begging to cross to this peaceful place.

My body a shocking moment.
Home sick in a momentum.
Its pain that cannot be wept.
So I stop, a personal vigil.

Deep breath, slowly..
Trailing the life flow in,
To all places that need touch.
To feel what bothers it sleepless.
To my discovery.
The tears of my pity soul not chanted.

Light & Dark

See us now.
See us no more.
The day rises us!
The night falls on us.
We are called in & out,
To be within & without
To see the life of light & dark.

Everything has the other side.
Turning, shifting.
changing everything.
We are up while down.
We laugh to cry...
We wish to receive.

We experience lessons!
While thinking to imagine.
Thought to realize,
That Love is light
Emerging from the dark.
It's all You!

Ancestor

Looking into the mirror.
Tell me what do you see.
A reflection
That originate the universe.

From above shinning stars,
To the deep still oceans reefs.
Your spirit hovers,
Instilling knowledge life
Love the purpose
For everything being.

You not dated by Time
You embedded in a petite connection
That pulls the wheelwagon of life
From the deathly hallows!

Everything exists at a point of return.
A prime cycle of eternity.
Where death seed Life.
You're the frequency that vibe alive.
Speaking the language of life.

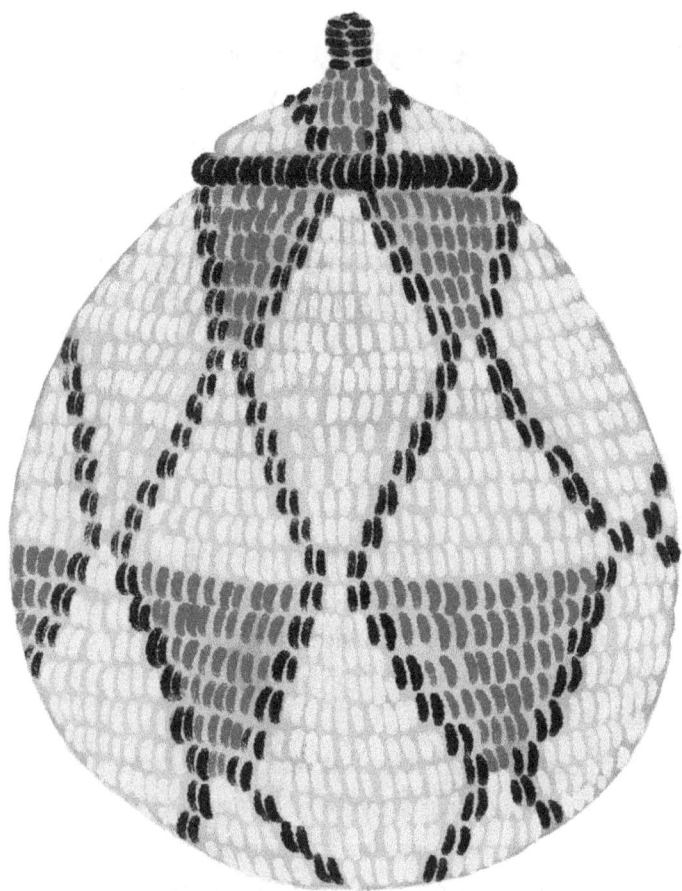

Deceived

We all came knowing
And all that we ignored.
As it burnt in hell.

There they are!
Men in white collars.
Walking gentle.
On a sweet melody.

They are holding crosses on the left hand,
That double crossed our
Hearts and minds
And a book of evil seduction on the right.

They calling on whorely teachings.
It cramp our stomachs,
So we spewed the love we deserve.

We left rattling, homeless
Begging to be saved,
As we pray on their promise,
Of everlasting life,
That cannot be fulfilled.
But ever ending our livelihood.

They are partaking on the promise land.
We partake on tribulations.
This fear kept our eyes closed!
Closed in hope to open to paradise.

When revelation rise.
We saw what they meant,
When they quoted
'Fear the lord, for he is the consuming fire!'
Indeed we Lambs,
Feasts The Shepard.

Heart and mind Armageddon

Divine is the heart with love
That dwells in knowledge
And one that delivers to good.
Through that small voice within
That intuition is the purpose
Purporting from your star

It is the window, portal
Pouring harmony within then without
Making a world a better stay
The heart is the path
To heaven we seek
Every time we close our eyes

Without the heart my dear,
No one can know
Or have sense of heaven's existence
But heart is the only way.

The heart is the wills way,
A way that is less travelled,
Only tapped by minority,the undermined,
The backwards In the world's countryside.

But the Mind is the projector that introduces one
To falseness, fear, hate
and finally exposing one to hell.

Appropriately the Mind is the believer of hell
A road trampled by magnitudes,
Walking, driving, feeding on ego.
Leading to souls demise.

Know thyself
are you for thy heart or mind,
Are you a believer or a knower?

Being a believer is deceiving,
And descending many
To a road of a Mind that is doubting!

While being a knower is fulfilling
Willing, pouring knowledge, .
Resurrection of thyself
Ascension to self-discovery,
A Realization that Made us Gods.

So do not lose love at your heart
Because if you do
You cannot find your way back home.
~ Tiyiselani Tlhavani

Truth

Truth as no companion.
Truth has no lawyer to stand for it in a courtroom.
Truth battles alone in the war zone.
Truth as no fans, no one is ever cheering for it.
Truth is a loner.

Truth is not married, no one is kissing it forever!
Truth dwells in caves, in darkness,
Not so welcome in modern life.
Truth is feared by many but not scary.
Politicians bait on it
Satan cannot find it in his mouth.

Truth always loved to be heard, uttered & inhabit the heart.
Truth always loved to be discussed by men & passed on to
the new generation.
Truth always gave us genuine smiles to laughs,
That hurt us but thereafter satisfied
Truth is the keeper, the good shepherd of life.

Truth you are forever missed, the earth's
ecosystem misses you!
Today you're forever hated & denied by many,
Many are dying, many are sick,
many are psychopaths because they didn't know you.

You're a giant that shouts in the public square,
crying for recognition,
Trying to be visible in every possible dimension,
But many had closed their eyes, lamented their ears,
Hating you for being crime-less, for being the keeper of love.
Truth you're on your own.

Truth you were always a good Shepard,
Guiding us through morality to immortality.
You were the reverend of our time.
You were the vehicle that put us through many generations,
Your UBUNTU cannot be forgotten that kept us together
As like firewood that work together
To prepare a Feast for a great celebration,
You were there in our midst,
We were champions, king & queens.
Truth today you're on your own.

QUOTES

A Heart is a champion!
But that is denied & doubted by many,
Along with its greatest spear we call love.
And shield we call morals.

Stay in touch with thy heart,
Do not let the mind lead you astray.

Mind thinks of the enemy,
Heart feels friends around.

The most beautiful thing that the world seek,
Reside within each one of us at HEART.
So, explore it, feel it
And spread it
And the world would be HEAVEN again

LOVE remains as the only Saviour of this trembling Temple
(body) of God (soul)
in this Chaotic space (world) ran by the Minds (believers).

A Lie is a poison of a mind
And Fear is the greatest the guard to keep it stronger!

Amid of silence,
The soul becomes a teacher/driver
And the mind becomes a listener/passenger at the back sit,

So love thy silence
And journey your mind to roads less travelled
And destinations not visited.

You wonder on the stars in the sky
While the stars wonders down on you.
So above & is as below,
We are the Wonders of the Universe.

Heaven is not so above our heads
but below right at the centre of our heart,
So navigate your paradise now.
Surrender your Mind to your heart and know love.
Shunning away from the Mind that believe in hate,
Fear and sorrow.

This Time & Space is a War zone.
Bodies keep on rising to fall,
Eye see to be blind,
Ear hears to be deaf,
Tongue speaks to be mute,

And the heart beats to be silent.
Only Soul keeps on flowing,
Rising forever!

It is realization that brought us here,
and we found ourselves caught in the eyes
by this enormous glittering light,
that poured, anointed us with divine energy
To See, feel, hear, touch and then smell.
Senses of knowledge/Love.
We are the beings of Light,
Without Light, We are finite.

You see me shine during the day
Also see me beam during the night.
Everything that you see, feel, hear and smell
Are merely corridors to meet/know yourself.

—◇—

The universe is not strange
The universe is yourself that you have not discovered.
Stop being strange to youniverse.
Know thyself.

—◇—

You hold the universe by eye
Hold its knowledge by brain
Hold its love by heart
Yet hold its wonders by the mind
And finally, you travel its magnitudes by soul.

Stay in balance,
You are the bride
And the groom of the universe
We are in cosmic marriage
Marriage that cannot be divorced

In our heart we knew
But in our mind we doubted
And in our eyes we wept!

Someone should stop weeping.!!
For Love to be realized in this world
The mind must swallow its ego
And bow down unto the heart.

Soul you're a divine teacher
That money cannot reward
A result that made many breath
A teacher that resurrects dust
Into balance, motion and
Meaningful Love
We call Life.

Heart is the mind of heaven within you.
So, whoever mind his heart now.
Later would be reminded heaven.

Silence is the frequency of knowledge,
That meditators seek to listen.
So they are let to know the message from the divine.

Guard your Love at heart with morals, because Greed is revving for it

When I avail myself to you
Do not judge me by the art of my mind
but define me by the art of my heart.
Because my mind is a property,
That can be hired, manipulated by entities
but in my heart is will, soul purpose
That defines my true self.

It is the mind that scatters the
Universe into pieces
And you see difference,
Separation,
Individualism that triggers ego

---

but it is the heart that seek to unite the
universe into Oneness
And You see same,
Connection,
Unity that shares humility

In mind we are different
In heart we are same,
The mind can judge
but heart cannot.

Love is what can only unite everything.
Everything within the universe have sense of love,
Sense of belonging,
To unite it back to its source.

So do not lose love at your heart
Because if you do
You cannot find your way back home.

In heart we are warm
But in hate we are cold,
As warm-blooded people
Are we ready to be set/
Cast on cold by this war?

Are we not going to shiver!
Perish in this cold room of hate?
Have you seen someone who is possessed by Cold,
Too much greed, too much ego.

I'm not of the hate nation,
Just set my spirit on fire
And see me rise and rise

The great wars are not fought on
Time and Space
But they are fought right within the
centre of our universe, HEART
Where everything is united under
the name LOVE.
This is where the war is fought to
dismantle, separate
And break away every unity it is
And then set it into mortality.

Tiyiselani Tlhavani 2025